EMMANUEL JOSEPH

The Eternal Ledger, Transforming International Business with Digital Currency

Copyright © 2025 by Emmanuel Joseph

All rights reserved. No part of this publication may be reproduced, stored or transmitted in any form or by any means, electronic, mechanical, photocopying, recording, scanning, or otherwise without written permission from the publisher. It is illegal to copy this book, post it to a website, or distribute it by any other means without permission.

First edition

This book was professionally typeset on Reedsy. Find out more at reedsy.com

Contents

1. Chapter 1: The Dawn of Digital Currency — 1
2. Chapter 2: The Rise of Blockchain Technology — 3
3. Chapter 3: The Adoption of Bitcoin — 5
4. Chapter 4: Ethereum and Smart Contracts — 7
5. Chapter 5: Regulatory Landscape — 9
6. Chapter 6: Digital Currency and Financial Inclusion — 11
7. Chapter 7: Cross-Border Transactions — 13
8. Chapter 8: The Role of Central Banks — 15
9. Chapter 9: Security and Privacy Concerns — 17
10. Chapter 10: Digital Currency and E-Commerce — 19
11. Chapter 11: The Future of Digital Currency — 21
12. Chapter 12: Conclusion: Embracing the Future — 23

1

Chapter 1: The Dawn of Digital Currency

The dawn of digital currency heralded a transformative era in the world of international business. Before its advent, transactions were often burdened by inefficiencies, delays, and the complexities of currency exchanges. However, the introduction of digital currency reshaped the landscape, promising a more streamlined and efficient global economy. As businesses across the globe began to adopt these innovative financial tools, the potential for seamless transactions and enhanced financial inclusion became increasingly evident. This chapter explores the early days of digital currency, highlighting its origins and the initial impact on international trade.

The concept of digital currency was not entirely new, with early attempts dating back to the late 20th century. However, it was the emergence of blockchain technology that truly revolutionized the field. Blockchain, a decentralized ledger system, provided the foundation for secure and transparent transactions. This innovation addressed the longstanding issues of trust and security that had plagued traditional financial systems. As businesses and governments began to recognize the potential of blockchain, the adoption of digital currencies like Bitcoin and later Ethereum gained momentum.

The initial reaction to digital currency was mixed, with some embracing it as the future of finance, while others remained skeptical. Critics pointed to the volatility and lack of regulation as potential pitfalls. Despite these concerns, early adopters saw the advantages of reduced transaction costs, faster cross-border payments, and the elimination of intermediaries. These benefits were particularly appealing to small and medium-sized enterprises (SMEs) that often faced challenges accessing traditional banking services. As more businesses experimented with digital currency, its role in facilitating international trade became increasingly apparent.

One of the most significant early applications of digital currency in international business was in remittances. Workers sending money back to their home countries found that digital currency offered a faster, cheaper, and more secure alternative to traditional methods. This development had profound implications for developing economies, where remittances constituted a substantial portion of GDP. As digital currency continued to evolve, its potential to drive economic growth and financial inclusion became a central theme. The dawn of digital currency marked the beginning of a new chapter in the history of international business, setting the stage for further innovations and transformations.

2

Chapter 2: The Rise of Blockchain Technology

Blockchain technology emerged as the backbone of digital currencies, offering a decentralized and secure method for recording transactions. Unlike traditional financial systems that rely on central authorities, blockchain operates on a distributed ledger system where every participant has access to the entire transaction history. This transparency ensures that transactions are verifiable and tamper-proof, significantly reducing the risk of fraud. In the early days, blockchain was primarily associated with cryptocurrencies like Bitcoin, but its potential applications soon extended far beyond digital currencies.

One of the key features of blockchain technology is its ability to facilitate trust in a trustless environment. In traditional financial systems, intermediaries like banks and clearinghouses are needed to establish trust between parties. However, blockchain's cryptographic principles and consensus mechanisms eliminate the need for these intermediaries. Transactions are validated by a network of nodes, ensuring that every participant agrees on the state of the ledger. This not only reduces transaction costs but also speeds up the settlement process, making cross-border transactions more efficient.

The rise of blockchain technology also brought about the concept of smart contracts. These self-executing contracts with the terms of the agreement directly written into code revolutionized the way businesses operate. Smart contracts automate complex business processes, reducing the need for manual intervention and minimizing the risk of human error. For example, in international trade, smart contracts can automatically trigger payments when certain conditions are met, such as the delivery of goods. This automation streamlines operations, enhances transparency, and increases trust between trading partners.

Beyond its financial applications, blockchain technology has the potential to transform various industries. Supply chain management, for instance, can greatly benefit from blockchain's ability to provide real-time visibility and traceability of goods. By recording every step of the supply chain on a blockchain, businesses can ensure the authenticity and quality of their products, reduce counterfeiting, and improve inventory management. Additionally, blockchain's impact on sectors like healthcare, real estate, and voting systems is beginning to unfold, showcasing its versatility and far-reaching implications.

3

Chapter 3: The Adoption of Bitcoin

The creation of Bitcoin by the pseudonymous Satoshi Nakamoto in 2008 marked a pivotal moment in the history of digital currency. Bitcoin was introduced as a peer-to-peer electronic cash system, promising a decentralized alternative to traditional financial systems. Its underlying technology, blockchain, allowed for secure and transparent transactions without the need for intermediaries. This innovation quickly captured the imagination of tech enthusiasts and early adopters, who saw the potential for a new era of digital finance. Bitcoin's open-source nature and the scarcity built into its protocol further fueled its allure.

The initial reception of Bitcoin was a mix of enthusiasm and skepticism. Early adopters, often referred to as "crypto pioneers," were intrigued by the potential for a currency that was not subject to the control of central banks or governments. They saw Bitcoin as a revolutionary tool for financial freedom and privacy. However, mainstream acceptance was slow to follow, as concerns about volatility, security, and regulatory uncertainty loomed large. Bitcoin's association with illicit activities on the dark web, such as the infamous Silk Road marketplace, further hindered its reputation in the early years.

Despite the challenges, Bitcoin began to find its footing as a viable means of exchange. Businesses, particularly those operating in the tech and e-commerce sectors, started to accept Bitcoin as a form of payment. Notable examples include companies like Overstock and Microsoft, which recognized the potential for reaching a new customer base and reducing transaction fees. Bitcoin's borderless nature made it especially appealing for international transactions, where traditional banking systems often imposed significant delays and costs. This newfound utility contributed to Bitcoin's growing legitimacy and value.

As Bitcoin continued to gain traction, it also sparked the development of a broader cryptocurrency ecosystem. The success of Bitcoin inspired the creation of numerous altcoins, each with its unique features and use cases. This proliferation of digital currencies further validated the concept of decentralized finance and underscored the transformative potential of blockchain technology. While Bitcoin remains the most well-known and widely adopted cryptocurrency, its impact extends far beyond its market capitalization. It paved the way for a new financial paradigm, challenging conventional notions of money and finance.

4

Chapter 4: Ethereum and Smart Contracts

Ethereum, introduced by Vitalik Buterin in 2015, brought a new dimension to the world of digital currency with the concept of smart contracts. Unlike Bitcoin, which was primarily designed as a digital currency, Ethereum was envisioned as a decentralized platform for running smart contracts. These self-executing contracts, with the terms of the agreement directly written into code, enable automated and trustless transactions. This innovation opened up a myriad of possibilities for businesses, from automating routine processes to creating decentralized applications (dApps).

Smart contracts have the potential to revolutionize business processes by eliminating the need for intermediaries. In traditional business transactions, intermediaries such as banks, lawyers, and escrow services are required to facilitate trust between parties. However, smart contracts use blockchain technology to automatically execute and enforce agreements when predefined conditions are met. This not only reduces transaction costs but also minimizes the risk of fraud and disputes. For example, in supply chain management, a smart contract can automatically release payment once a shipment reaches its destination, ensuring timely and accurate payments.

The flexibility of the Ethereum platform has led to the development of a wide range of applications beyond financial transactions. Decentralized finance (DeFi) is one of the most significant and rapidly growing sectors within the Ethereum ecosystem. DeFi applications leverage smart contracts to create financial instruments such as loans, insurance, and exchanges without the need for traditional intermediaries. This democratizes access to financial services, especially for individuals and businesses in regions with limited banking infrastructure. The growth of DeFi has highlighted the transformative potential of smart contracts in reshaping the financial landscape.

Despite its promise, the adoption of Ethereum and smart contracts is not without challenges. Scalability remains a significant concern, as the Ethereum network can become congested during periods of high demand, leading to increased transaction fees and delays. Security is another critical issue, as vulnerabilities in smart contract code can be exploited by malicious actors. Nevertheless, ongoing research and development aim to address these challenges and enhance the capabilities of the Ethereum platform. The continuous evolution of Ethereum and its applications underscores the dynamic nature of the digital currency landscape and its potential to drive further innovation in international business.

5

Chapter 5: Regulatory Landscape

As digital currencies gained traction, governments and regulatory bodies around the world began to take notice. The rapid rise of cryptocurrencies like Bitcoin and Ethereum posed both opportunities and challenges for regulators. On one hand, digital currencies promised to enhance financial inclusion, reduce transaction costs, and foster innovation. On the other hand, they raised concerns about consumer protection, money laundering, and the stability of financial systems. This chapter delves into the evolving regulatory landscape for digital currencies and the efforts to strike a balance between fostering innovation and ensuring security.

Early regulatory responses to digital currencies varied widely across different jurisdictions. Some countries, such as Japan and Switzerland, embraced digital currencies and developed clear regulatory frameworks to support their growth. Japan, for example, recognized Bitcoin as a legal method of payment in 2017 and introduced licensing requirements for cryptocurrency exchanges. Switzerland, known for its crypto-friendly policies, established a regulatory framework that encouraged innovation while ensuring compliance with anti-money laundering (AML) and know-your-customer (KYC) regulations. These proactive approaches aimed to create a conducive environment for digital currency businesses while mitigating risks.

In contrast, other countries took a more cautious or restrictive stance towards digital currencies. China, for instance, imposed a ban on initial coin offerings (ICOs) and shut down domestic cryptocurrency exchanges in 2017, citing concerns about financial stability and fraud. The United States adopted a more nuanced approach, with different regulatory agencies providing guidance on various aspects of digital currency. The Securities and Exchange Commission (SEC) focused on ICOs and classified certain tokens as securities, while the Commodity Futures Trading Commission (CFTC) treated Bitcoin and other cryptocurrencies as commodities. This fragmented regulatory landscape created challenges for businesses operating across multiple jurisdictions.

International organizations also played a crucial role in shaping the regulatory landscape for digital currencies. The Financial Action Task Force (FATF), an intergovernmental body that sets standards for combating money laundering and terrorist financing, issued guidelines for regulating virtual assets and virtual asset service providers. These guidelines aimed to enhance global cooperation and ensure a consistent approach to AML and KYC compliance. The International Monetary Fund (IMF) and the World Bank also explored the implications of digital currencies for financial stability and economic development, providing valuable insights for policymakers.

As the regulatory landscape continues to evolve, the challenge for regulators is to strike a balance between fostering innovation and ensuring the safety and integrity of financial systems. While stringent regulations can stifle innovation, a lack of oversight can expose consumers and businesses to significant risks. Collaborative efforts between regulators, industry stakeholders, and international organizations are essential to develop effective and balanced regulatory frameworks. The ongoing dialogue between these entities will shape the future of digital currencies and their role in the global economy.

6

Chapter 6: Digital Currency and Financial Inclusion

Digital currency holds significant promise for enhancing financial inclusion, particularly in regions where access to traditional banking services is limited. In many developing countries, a substantial portion of the population remains unbanked or underbanked, lacking access to essential financial services such as savings accounts, credit, and insurance. Digital currencies, along with mobile banking technologies, offer a viable solution to bridge this gap and provide financial services to those who need them most. This chapter explores the impact of digital currency on financial inclusion and highlights successful initiatives that have leveraged this technology.

One of the primary advantages of digital currency is its ability to reach remote and underserved populations. Mobile phones have become ubiquitous in many developing regions, providing a convenient platform for accessing digital financial services. Digital wallets, for example, enable individuals to store, send, and receive money using their mobile devices. This accessibility empowers people to participate in the formal economy, make secure transactions, and build financial resilience. Furthermore, digital currency can facilitate microtransactions and micropayments, allowing individuals to access goods and services that were previously out of reach due to high transaction costs.

Several case studies demonstrate the transformative impact of digital currency on financial inclusion. In Kenya, the mobile money platform M-Pesa has revolutionized financial services, providing millions of people with access to banking services through their mobile phones. M-Pesa's success has inspired similar initiatives in other countries, showcasing the potential of digital currency to drive financial inclusion. In the Philippines, the blockchain-based platform Coins.ph has enabled individuals to access financial services, pay bills, and transfer money using digital currency. These examples highlight the potential of digital currency to empower individuals and communities, fostering economic growth and development.

The role of digital currency in promoting financial inclusion extends beyond individual users to small and medium-sized enterprises (SMEs). SMEs often face significant challenges in accessing credit and financial services due to high transaction costs and limited collateral. Digital currency and blockchain technology can streamline these processes, reducing barriers to entry and providing SMEs with access to essential financial resources. For instance, blockchain-based lending platforms can facilitate peer-to-peer lending, allowing SMEs to secure funding from a global pool of investors. By enhancing financial inclusion, digital currency can drive entrepreneurship, innovation, and economic development in underserved regions.

7

Chapter 7: Cross-Border Transactions

Cross-border transactions have traditionally been a complex and costly affair, involving multiple intermediaries, currency conversions, and compliance with various regulatory frameworks. Digital currency, however, has the potential to simplify and streamline these processes, making international trade more efficient and accessible. This chapter explores the challenges of traditional cross-border transactions and how digital currency addresses these issues, offering case studies of businesses that have successfully leveraged digital currency for international trade.

Traditional cross-border payments are often plagued by delays and high costs. Transactions can take several days to settle, with each intermediary adding fees and potential points of failure. Currency conversion adds another layer of complexity, as exchange rates fluctuate and banks charge additional fees for conversion services. These inefficiencies are particularly burdensome for small and medium-sized enterprises (SMEs), which may lack the resources to navigate the intricacies of international finance. Digital currency offers a solution by enabling direct peer-to-peer transactions without the need for intermediaries, reducing both costs and settlement times.

One of the key advantages of digital currency in cross-border transactions is its borderless nature. Digital currencies like Bitcoin and stablecoins can be transferred globally with minimal friction, bypassing traditional banking channels and avoiding currency conversion fees. This is especially beneficial for businesses operating in multiple countries or dealing with international suppliers and customers. For instance, a business in Nigeria can easily send payments to a supplier in China using digital currency, without worrying about exchange rates or intermediary fees. This streamlined process enhances liquidity and facilitates faster and more efficient trade.

Several case studies illustrate the transformative impact of digital currency on cross-border transactions. For example, a European e-commerce company began accepting Bitcoin as a payment method, allowing customers from around the world to make purchases without the need for credit cards or bank accounts. This not only expanded the company's customer base but also reduced transaction costs and chargeback risks. In another example, a remittance service provider used stablecoins to facilitate low-cost cross-border transfers for migrant workers, ensuring that more of their hard-earned money reached their families back home. These case studies highlight the potential of digital currency to revolutionize international trade and financial services.

As digital currency continues to gain traction in cross-border transactions, the future looks promising. Emerging technologies such as blockchain-based payment networks and central bank digital currencies (CBDCs) hold the potential to further enhance the efficiency and security of international payments. However, challenges such as regulatory uncertainty, scalability, and interoperability must be addressed to fully realize the benefits of digital currency in cross-border trade. Collaborative efforts between businesses, regulators, and technology providers will be crucial in shaping the future of international finance and ensuring that digital currency continues to drive innovation and inclusion.

8

Chapter 8: The Role of Central Banks

The rise of digital currency has prompted central banks around the world to reconsider their roles in the financial system. Traditionally, central banks have been responsible for issuing currency, regulating monetary policy, and maintaining financial stability. However, the emergence of decentralized digital currencies challenges the traditional notion of money and raises questions about the future of central banking. This chapter explores the evolving role of central banks in the age of digital currency, focusing on the concept of Central Bank Digital Currencies (CBDCs) and their potential impact on the global financial system.

Central banks' initial reactions to digital currency were cautious, with many expressing concerns about the implications for monetary policy and financial stability. The decentralized nature of cryptocurrencies like Bitcoin posed a challenge to the traditional control that central banks exert over the money supply. Additionally, the potential for digital currencies to facilitate illicit activities and evade regulatory oversight raised further apprehensions. Despite these concerns, the rapid adoption of digital currency and the growing interest from the public and private sectors prompted central banks to explore the possibilities and implications of issuing their digital currencies.

The concept of Central Bank Digital Currencies (CBDCs) emerged as a potential solution to the challenges posed by decentralized digital currencies. CBDCs are digital forms of a country's sovereign currency, issued and regulated by the central bank. Unlike cryptocurrencies, CBDCs are centralized and operate within the existing regulatory framework. Central banks envision CBDCs as a way to enhance the efficiency and security of payment systems, promote financial inclusion, and ensure the stability of the monetary system. Several countries, including China, Sweden, and the Bahamas, have already piloted or launched their CBDC projects, showcasing the potential benefits and challenges of this new form of money.

The introduction of CBDCs could have far-reaching implications for the global financial system. For one, CBDCs could revolutionize cross-border payments by reducing the reliance on correspondent banks and streamlining the settlement process. This would not only lower transaction costs but also enhance the speed and transparency of international transactions. Additionally, CBDCs could promote financial inclusion by providing unbanked and underbanked populations with access to digital financial services. However, the widespread adoption of CBDCs also raises concerns about privacy, cybersecurity, and the potential for central banks to exert greater control over the financial system.

As central banks continue to explore the possibilities of CBDCs, collaboration and dialogue with other stakeholders will be essential. The successful implementation of CBDCs will require a coordinated effort between central banks, financial institutions, technology providers, and policymakers. By working together, these entities can address the technical, regulatory, and ethical challenges associated with CBDCs and unlock the potential benefits for the global economy. The evolving role of central banks in the age of digital currency underscores the need for innovation, adaptability, and cooperation in navigating the future of finance.

9

Chapter 9: Security and Privacy Concerns

As digital currencies become more prevalent in international business, concerns about security and privacy have come to the forefront. The decentralized and pseudonymous nature of digital currencies presents both opportunities and challenges in this regard. While blockchain technology inherently offers a high level of security through its cryptographic principles, it is not entirely immune to threats. This chapter delves into the key security and privacy concerns associated with digital currency, highlighting the importance of safeguarding transactions and protecting user data.

One of the primary security concerns with digital currency is the risk of hacking and cyberattacks. Cryptocurrency exchanges, wallets, and other platforms have been targeted by hackers seeking to steal digital assets. High-profile incidents, such as the Mt. Gox hack in 2014, where approximately 850,000 Bitcoins were stolen, underscore the vulnerabilities within the ecosystem. To mitigate these risks, businesses and users must implement robust security measures, including multi-factor authentication, cold storage solutions, and regular security audits. Additionally, advancements in cryptographic techniques and the development of secure protocols continue to enhance the resilience of digital currency systems.

Privacy is another critical issue in the digital currency space. While blockchain transactions are transparent and publicly accessible, they are pseudonymous, meaning that users' real identities are not directly linked to their wallet addresses. However, sophisticated techniques can be used to deanonymize users and trace their transactions. Privacy-focused cryptocurrencies, such as Monero and Zcash, have emerged to address these concerns by offering enhanced privacy features. These cryptocurrencies utilize advanced cryptographic methods, such as ring signatures and zero-knowledge proofs, to obfuscate transaction details and protect user identities. As privacy concerns grow, businesses and individuals must be aware of the trade-offs between transparency and privacy in their use of digital currency.

In addition to external threats, internal risks such as human error and insider attacks also pose significant challenges. Employees with access to sensitive information or control over digital assets can inadvertently or maliciously compromise security. Implementing strict access controls, conducting regular training, and fostering a culture of security awareness are essential steps in mitigating these risks. Moreover, the use of smart contracts and automated systems can reduce the reliance on human intervention and minimize the potential for errors and misconduct. However, the security of smart contracts themselves must be rigorously assessed to prevent vulnerabilities and exploits.

As the digital currency landscape continues to evolve, ongoing efforts to address security and privacy concerns are crucial. Collaboration between industry stakeholders, regulators, and technology providers is essential to develop and implement best practices and standards. Regulatory frameworks that strike a balance between innovation and security can help build trust and confidence in digital currencies. By prioritizing security and privacy, businesses and users can fully leverage the benefits of digital currency while safeguarding their assets and information.

10

Chapter 10: Digital Currency and E-Commerce

The rapid growth of e-commerce has created a demand for faster, more secure, and cost-effective payment solutions. Traditional payment methods, such as credit cards and bank transfers, often come with high fees, long settlement times, and the risk of fraud. Digital currency offers a compelling alternative, addressing these challenges and providing a seamless payment experience for both consumers and merchants. This chapter explores the role of digital currency in e-commerce, highlighting its benefits, challenges, and future trends.

One of the primary advantages of digital currency in e-commerce is the reduction of transaction costs. Traditional payment methods involve multiple intermediaries, each taking a cut of the transaction value. Digital currency transactions, on the other hand, are peer-to-peer and can be conducted with minimal fees. This is particularly beneficial for small and medium-sized enterprises (SMEs), which often operate on tight margins. By accepting digital currency, e-commerce businesses can reduce their payment processing costs and offer more competitive prices to their customers.

Another significant benefit of digital currency is the speed of transactions. Traditional payment methods can take several days to settle, especially for international transactions. Digital currency transactions are typically processed within minutes, providing immediate confirmation and reducing the risk of chargebacks. This is especially advantageous for cross-border e-commerce, where delays and currency conversion fees can be a major hindrance. The ability to conduct fast and frictionless transactions enhances the overall customer experience and builds trust between buyers and sellers.

However, the adoption of digital currency in e-commerce is not without challenges. One of the main concerns is the volatility of cryptocurrencies like Bitcoin, which can lead to significant fluctuations in the value of payments. To mitigate this risk, some businesses prefer to use stablecoins, which are pegged to fiat currencies and offer price stability. Additionally, the regulatory landscape for digital currency is still evolving, and businesses must navigate compliance requirements to ensure they operate within the legal framework. Security is another critical issue, as digital wallets and exchanges can be vulnerable to hacking and fraud. Implementing robust security measures and educating customers about safe practices are essential steps to protect digital assets.

As the e-commerce industry continues to evolve, the integration of digital currency is expected to grow. Emerging technologies such as blockchain-based payment gateways and decentralized marketplaces hold the potential to further revolutionize the way online transactions are conducted. Moreover, the increasing acceptance of digital currency by major retailers and payment processors signals a shift towards mainstream adoption. As more consumers and businesses recognize the benefits of digital currency, its role in e-commerce is likely to expand, driving innovation and transforming the digital economy.

11

Chapter 11: The Future of Digital Currency

The future of digital currency is a topic of considerable interest and speculation. As technology continues to advance, the potential applications and implications of digital currency are likely to expand in ways we can only begin to imagine. This chapter explores some of the key trends and predictions for the evolution of digital currency, highlighting emerging technologies, potential challenges, and opportunities for businesses and governments.

One of the most promising trends in the digital currency space is the integration of blockchain technology with the Internet of Things (IoT). The convergence of these technologies could enable seamless and automated transactions between connected devices, creating a new paradigm for commerce. For example, IoT-enabled supply chains could use blockchain-based smart contracts to automatically trigger payments and update records as goods move through the production and distribution process. This would enhance transparency, reduce the risk of fraud, and improve efficiency. Additionally, IoT devices could use digital currency for microtransactions, enabling new business models and revenue streams.

Another emerging trend is the development of decentralized finance (DeFi) platforms. DeFi leverages blockchain technology to create financial services and products without the need for traditional intermediaries. This includes lending and borrowing, trading, insurance, and more. DeFi has the potential to democratize access to financial services, particularly for individuals and businesses in regions with limited banking infrastructure. However, the rapid growth of DeFi also raises concerns about security, scalability, and regulatory compliance. As the DeFi ecosystem continues to evolve, it will be important to address these challenges and ensure that the benefits of decentralized finance are accessible to all.

The rise of stablecoins and central bank digital currencies (CBDCs) is another key trend that will shape the future of digital currency. Stablecoins, which are pegged to fiat currencies, offer the benefits of digital currency while minimizing the volatility associated with cryptocurrencies like Bitcoin. CBDCs, on the other hand, represent a new form of sovereign currency issued by central banks. Both stablecoins and CBDCs have the potential to enhance the efficiency and inclusivity of the global financial system. However, their widespread adoption will require collaboration between regulators, financial institutions, and technology providers to address issues related to governance, privacy, and interoperability.

As digital currency continues to evolve, it will be essential for businesses and governments to stay informed and adapt to the changing landscape. The successful integration of digital currency into the global economy will depend on a balanced approach that fosters innovation while ensuring security and compliance. By embracing the opportunities presented by digital currency and addressing the associated challenges, we can create a more inclusive, efficient, and resilient financial system. The future of digital currency is bright, and its potential to transform international business is only beginning to be realized.

12

Chapter 12: Conclusion: Embracing the Future

The journey of digital currency from a nascent concept to a transformative force in international business has been nothing short of remarkable. This book has explored the various dimensions of digital currency, from its origins and technological foundations to its applications and regulatory challenges. The promise of digital currency lies not only in its ability to enhance efficiency and reduce costs but also in its potential to foster financial inclusion and drive innovation. As we look to the future, it is essential for businesses, governments, and individuals to embrace the opportunities presented by digital currency while addressing the associated risks and challenges.

One of the key takeaways from this exploration is the importance of collaboration and cooperation. The successful integration of digital currency into the global economy will require a concerted effort from all stakeholders. Businesses must stay informed about the latest developments and be willing to adapt their strategies to leverage digital currency effectively. Governments and regulators must strike a balance between fostering innovation and ensuring the safety and integrity of financial systems. Technology providers must continue to develop secure and scalable solutions that meet the needs of a diverse range of users. By working together, we can create a more inclusive, efficient, and resilient financial system.

Innovation and adaptability are also crucial as we navigate the future of digital currency. The landscape is constantly evolving, with new technologies and trends emerging at a rapid pace. Businesses and individuals must be agile and open to change, embracing new opportunities and overcoming challenges as they arise. The potential applications of digital currency are vast, spanning various industries and use cases. From cross-border transactions and supply chain management to decentralized finance and e-commerce, digital currency has the power to transform the way we conduct business and interact with the global economy.

In conclusion, the future of digital currency is bright, and its impact on international business is only beginning to be realized. The journey ahead will undoubtedly be filled with both opportunities and challenges, but the potential rewards are significant. By embracing digital currency and leveraging its capabilities, we can unlock new levels of efficiency, inclusivity, and innovation. As we move forward, it is essential to remain vigilant, informed, and proactive in addressing the evolving landscape of digital currency. Together, we can shape the future of international business and create a more prosperous and interconnected world.

The Eternal Ledger: Transforming International Business with Digital Currency

"The Eternal Ledger: Transforming International Business with Digital Currency" is an insightful exploration into the revolutionary impact of digital currency on global commerce. This comprehensive book delves into the origins of digital currencies, the rise of blockchain technology, and the pivotal role of cryptocurrencies like Bitcoin and Ethereum in reshaping the financial landscape. Through twelve engaging chapters, readers are taken on a journey from the early days of digital currency to the present and future implications for international business.

The book covers a wide array of topics, including the technological foundations of blockchain, the regulatory landscape, and the potential for digital currency to enhance financial inclusion and streamline cross-border transactions. It examines the innovative concept of smart contracts and their

CHAPTER 12: CONCLUSION: EMBRACING THE FUTURE

applications in automating business processes, as well as the role of Central Bank Digital Currencies (CBDCs) in the evolving monetary system. With real-world case studies and practical insights, "The Eternal Ledger" showcases how businesses can leverage digital currency to reduce costs, increase efficiency, and drive innovation.

Written in an accessible and engaging style, this book is suitable for both newcomers and seasoned professionals in the fields of finance, technology, and international trade. It provides a balanced perspective on the opportunities and challenges associated with digital currency, offering readers a deeper understanding of its transformative potential. Whether you are a business leader, policy maker, or simply curious about the future of money, "The Eternal Ledger" is an essential guide to navigating the dynamic world of digital currency and its impact on global business.

www.ingramcontent.com/pod-product-compliance
Lightning Source LLC
LaVergne TN
LVHW020744090526
838202LV00057BA/6221